D1195149

SEURAT

PHAIDON

STUDY FOR 'THE CIRCUS'. 1890. Paris, Musée d'Art Moderne

SEURAT

WITH AN ESSAY BY ROGER FRY
AND A FOREWORD & NOTES BY
SIR ANTHONY BLUNT

FIFTY PLATES IN FULL COLOUR

PHAIDON PUBLISHERS INC
DISTRIBUTED BY
NEW YORK GRAPHIC SOCIETY PUBLISHERS LTD
GREENWICH · CONNECTICUT

LONDON · 1965

PLATES PRINTED BY V.S.K. PRINTERS · BASLE

TEXT PRINTED BY HUNT BARNARD & CO. LTD · AT THE SIGN OF THE DOLPHIN

AYLESBURY · BUCKINGHAMSHIRE · ENGLAND

FOREWORD

TO THE GENERATION that was growing up in the 1920's, when Roger Fry was at the height of his career, the most influential part of his writings was that series of speculative essays in which he set forth his aesthetic theories. These he had evolved to explain and to rationalize the deep admiration which had been aroused in him by the work of certain late nineteenth and early twentieth century French painters, to whom he gave the generic name of Post-Impressionists. He was a prophet who, having discovered an aspect of beauty to which most of his fellow-countrymen were blind, was determined to open their eyes to it and quite literally to convert them to his own convictions.

'Prophet' is the appropriate word to describe Fry, for, although he was himself a strong free-thinker, his Quaker ancestry had a powerful influence on his mode of thought and gave it a character which was not far from religious enthusiasm. This was most strikingly apparent in his lectures; his appearance, his voice, his whole manner produced a feeling of awe in his listeners; when he talked about an artist whom he loved, the scales literally fell from one's eyes; and when he was dealing with a form of art of which he disapproved, though one might disagree, the impression was equally strong: it was like listening to Jonah cursing the Ninevites.

Fry, however, was a scientist by training, not a philosopher, and, viewed from a distance of forty years, some of his theories seem less persuasive than they did at the time. This is perhaps an unimportant and certainly a temporary criticism; for, when they were put forward, the theories served their purpose – to break down traditional aesthetic beliefs which prevented us from understanding the Post-Impressionists – and in a century they will be valued as among the clearest and most honest statements of a doctrine that was vitally significant during the first quarter of the twentieth century.

Fry never pursued speculation for its own sake; his theories were produced as explanations for what he had seen and felt; and both his eyes and his sensibility were quite unusually perceptive. His knowledge of works of art and his range of appreciation were both vast. He had blind spots – a refusal to recognize the qualities of Greek art was probably the most serious – but at one period or another of his life he studied and enjoyed an astonishing number of works of art of the most diverse kinds. Starting on perfectly conventional lines with a highly scholarly knowledge of Italian Renaissance painting and a respect for the giants of the seventeenth century – Rembrandt, Rubens, Velazquez and Poussin – he was among the first English critics to write with understanding of El Greco, of Italian baroque painting, of so-called Primitive art, whether African, South American or Oceanian, and in his last years his deepest love was probably for the art of China and Persia; but his name will always be linked with the 'discovery' of French late nineteenth-century painting. As he himself readily admitted, he was far from being first in the field; certain enlightened French collectors had realized the genius of Cézanne, Van Gogh and their contemporaries a generation before Fry came to know them; their works had begun to be collected in Central Europe and even in America; and some interest had been shown in them by isolated enthusiasts in this country. But the fact remains that it was Fry and his friends who fought the battle to get the Post-Impressionists recognized in England, and though the exhibitions of 1910 and 1912 may seem in retrospect peculiar in their selection and unbalanced in their emphasis, they, together with the missionary work with which Fry and his friends accompanied them, broke the ice and prepared the way for the real understanding of an art which at that time was viewed with hostility and ridicule by most English critics.

It is probably the essays, some short, some longer, which Fry wrote on individual Post-Impressionist painters that will give us today the best idea of his qualities as a critic. In these his power of observation, his absolute humility and integrity in front of a work of art, and his ability to dissect his emotions without destroying their intensity in the process appear to the full and pure speculation plays a minor part, though in every case Fry seeks to arrive at general truths from his observations on individual artists.

Curiously enough Fry came to appreciate and love Post-Impressionist painting not through seeing the works of those painters who were eventually to be his real gods – Cézanne and Seurat – but through Gauguin, whom he later slightly frowned on as a Romantic, and Van Gogh, whom he was eventually to define – and this, from Fry, was a form of condemnation – as 'more an illustrator than a plastic artist'. His book on Cézanne – perhaps his most completely mature analysis of any artist – did not appear till 1927, and the essay on Seurat, printed below, was written to celebrate the acquisition by the Tate Gallery of the *Baignade* in 1924. In these two works Fry was faced with artists whom he admired and loved without qualification, and who did not raise within him all those troubling questions of theory which, though they make fascinating reading as examples of a highly intelligent mind trying to arrive at a precise definition of the truth, can sometimes be provoking to the modern reader. With Cézanne and Seurat Fry was not worried by the conflict between illustration and formal perfection; both artists were masters of plastic composition, though, as he pointed out, one derived his formal harmonies from a minute and humble contemplation of nature, whereas the other imposed on nature a rigid and preconceived system. Both Cézanne and Seurat had an intellectual integrity that satisfied an essential longing in Fry, for, although in theory he strove to dissociate aesthetics from ethics, his writings both on artists and on individual works of art are full of judgments which show that at bottom the two ideas cannot be wholly separated.

Nowadays we should probably not take such a strictly 'abstract' attitude towards the art of Seurat as that taken by Fry in the following essay and in the shorter one on *La Parade*, of which the essential parts are printed in the note on this picture (cf. below, pp. 83-84). It is true that Seurat produced some of the most perfectly satisfying formal designs since Piero della Francesca, and also that he evolved a highly self-conscious and intellectual method of execution (see below, p. 75), but it is also true – and this is a fact which Fry admits but of which he minimizes the importance – that his pictures represent in vivid form the life of the middle-classes of Paris and its suburbs in the 1880's. It would be foolish to read into his painting a social or political programme, but it cannot be a matter of chance that such a high proportion of his small early paintings represent subjects like stonebreakers or peasants at work in the fields. It is true that they are not treated with the violent compassion of a Van Gogh, or with the political consciousness of a Courbet, but they are equally far removed from the dispassionate curiosity with which Degas studied human beings in their various occupations; and it must not be forgotten that Seurat was a friend of Camille Pissarro, Félix Fénéon and others who were enthusiastic anarchists.

In Seurat's later works the problem is more complicated. The artist is certainly not putting forward any political or humanitarian thesis; on the other hand the *Baignade* conveys as vividly as can be the atmosphere of a hot summer afternoon on the river at Asnières in the 1880's – more vividly even than the stories of Maupassant, in spite of their sparkle, because there is not in Seurat that touch of malice which almost always distorts the great writer's vision. With the *Grande Jatte* we are carried a stage further. The observation is here detached, even amused, though it is hard for us to tell now whether or not Seurat realized and consciously stressed the comical outline of the bustles and the *art-nouveau* forms of the parasols. Here it is still a hot afternoon on the Seine, but the subject has been frozen into a sort of Egyptian frieze.

In *La Parade* the dream-like quality of the whole painting has grown stronger. The scene is still taken from ordinary life, but it is removed from it by the rigidity of the geometrical composition and by the extreme stylization of the actual handling. But both in this painting and in *Le Chahut* the human element cannot be disregarded; indeed in *Le Chahut* it is hard to believe that a point of satire was not intended.

Such considerations were however for Fry unimportant compared with the questions of formal harmony, in which Seurat's paintings are so pre-eminently successful, and although he observes them – and in his comments on *La Parade* observes them with humour – they are not for him an essential element in Seurat's greatness. Or rather – should one say? – they were not important for him at the time he wrote his two essays on this artist, for there is ample evidence to show that in his last years Fry was changing his approach towards painting and towards the basic principles of aesthetics. There are passages in his lecture on Rembrandt, recently published in *Apollo*, which show that he was once again concerned with the problem whether great illustration could be great art. In this case he still maintains, by implication, his old view, because he only admits Rembrandt to be a great painter in his last years, when, according to him, he had more or less ceased to be interested in 'illustration'. In his book on French painting, written on the occasion of the great exhibition at Burlington House in 1932, he seems to go further, and his analysis of the genre paintings of Chardin shows an understanding of the psychological subtleties of this artist that would make any 'traditional' critic jealous.

Within a very few years of his death in 1934 Fry's ideas were to be exposed to violent attack. Partly under the influence of Marxist aesthetics the younger generation were to react against his extreme statement of the 'pure form' doctrine; they felt – and not without reason – that Fry's view that the work of the great artist does not touch any of 'the finer issues of life' imposed a limitation on art which was not acceptable and that it left unexplained too many categories of works of art. It meant in effect dismissing as mere illustrators artists like Van Gogh in the near past, Rembrandt in the less remote past, and beyond that the whole art of the Middle Ages, as devoted to the service of religion instead of to the solving of purely plastic problems.

We were certainly violent in our reaction against Fry, but I have no doubt that, if he had still been alive, he would have enjoyed arguing with those who were attacking him; because, though he was a prophet, he never pontificated; he would always listen to the ideas of others, however young and however arrogant, and his own theories, which were certainly, so to speak, under review in his last years, might well have changed and have helped those younger than himself to arrive at a reasonable synthesis of their views and his own earlier ideas.

LONDON, 1965 ANTHONY BLUNT

GEORGES SEURAT

by Roger Fry

THE ACQUISITION by the Tate Gallery through the Courtauld Fund of Seurat's *Bathers* [Plate 15, now in the National Gallery], the purchase by an American for a high price of the *Grande-Jatte* [Plate 21, now in the Chicago Art Institute], the acquisition by the Louvre of *Le Cirque* [Plate 48], and lately an exhibition of his works at the Lefèvre Gallery [*Pictures and Drawings by Georges Seurat*, April - May 1926], all show that Seurat is at last coming into his inheritance. That he has not already done so long ago may at first sight seem surprising. It is due partly to the special character of Seurat's genius, partly to the accident that, just when he might have emerged, Cézanne, himself long overdue, occupied the field to the exclusion of every rival. But now that Cézanne's contribution has gradually been assimilated by the artistic consciousness of our day, it is evident that, if we set aside Renoir and Degas, whose work had long been accepted, the other outstanding figure of later nineteenth-century art is that of Seurat.

None the less he will, I think, always make rather a limited appeal. There was in his personality the strangest combination of an extreme sensibility and a devouring intellectual passion. He had, indeed, what is perhaps a good thing for an artist, more intellect than judgment. He had a passion for reducing the results of sensation to abstract statements, such, for instance, as his well-known formula of the effect of lines in composition, namely, that gaiety is given by lines ascending from the horizontal, calmness by horizontal lines, and sadness by descending lines. Gaiety, by the by, is about the last quality one would predicate of his *Cirque*, which is a deliberate demonstration of the effect of ascending lines. Such abstractions go but a very little way towards explaining the effect of so complex a thing as a pictorial design, still less can they be made much use of for the creation of such a complex. But it was a peculiarity of Seurat's intense love of method that it was by working along such lines as these that he was able, as it were, to lay by in pigeon-holes those actual sensations upon which his sensibility was nourished. Thus he proceeded perpetually by analysis and classification working out separately and in turn the effective qualities of line, tone and colour. When he came to synthesize, the process almost appeared to him to be a mere logical deduction from the classified data of sensation – a deduction which could be stated by perfectly ascertained and preconceived methods. He is even said to have carried these so far that he was able to work all night in a feeble gaslight covering his huge canvases with his innumerable dots of colour, so exactly was the effect of each of the colours which he had previously mixed, ascertained.

Nothing can be imagined more deliberate, more pre-ordained than this method, nothing less like that divine afflatus of inspiration with which artists are often credited. And yet inspiration is the word one has to use before such strangely original conceptions as his landscapes declare. Who before Seurat ever conceived exactly the pictorial possibilities of empty space? Whoever before conceived that such vast areas of flat, unbroken surfaces as we see in his *Gravelines* could become the elements of a plastic design? And yet nothing less 'empty,' pictorially speaking, can be imagined. There is such a tense, imaginative conviction in these subtly-built-up statements of surface that one can well believe that Seurat's own definition of the art of painting, as 'the art of hollowing out a canvas', was so evident to him as to make the effort of the imagination in cutting away so much material proportional to the vastness and emptiness of the space thus excavated.

And this work is accomplished solely by reason of such a delicate sensibility that it can perceive and hold firm almost infinitesimal changes of value. It is by the accumulation of these almost invisible gradations that the result is obtained. That incredibly laborious technique of a minute pointillism was perhaps the only possible technique that would admit of such subtlety of variation. This, indeed, seems to me to have been of even greater importance to Seurat's aim than the extra luminosity claimed for it. It alone allowed of a sufficiently slow and tentative approach to the final statement, it alone made evident the slightest changes of tone. Often, indeed, the whole structure of a design is held together by those slight changes of tone which are due to illusion, as when one sees the sky just a little darker where it comes against the edge of a white sail or a building. And yet, for all this close adherence to observation, how unlike anything natural these pictures are! How utterly fixed and immovable everything is! His pictures are alive, indeed, but not with the life of nature. He will paint air and almost nothing but air filled with light, but there is no breath in his air. If his designs live and breathe it is by the tension of the imaginative concentration which they reveal and impel us to share. Seurat is of the lineage of Poussin, and he is as austerely aloof and detached as he.

Seurat's ambition was as vast as his disinterestedness was complete. He attacked and carried through with a kind of inspired and yet ant-like patience the most terrifying pictorial problems. To conciliate those fleeting evanescent atmospheric effects which the Impressionists had noted in their rapid and fluent manner with the exacting canons of classic composition and to realize this completely on a large scale by the slow accumulation on the canvas of myriads of minute dots of colour might

DETAIL FROM 'WOMAN POWDERING HERSELF'.
Probably 1889–1890. London, Courtauld Institute Galleries (Home House Trustees)

Fig. 1: PORTRAIT OF SEURAT'S MOTHER. Drawing, about 1885. New York, Mr. and Mrs. Alex M. Lewyt

have deterred any one but a fanatic. And indeed there must have been something of a fanatical devotion beneath the rigorous intellect and reserved manner of this strange young man.

It was in the *Bathers* that he made the first grand demonstration of his new ideas. The scene is laid on the banks of the Seine just outside Paris. In the hot summer afternoon boys recline or sit, naked or partly dressed, on the bank with cast-off clothes and boots scattered on the grass, whilst others are playing in the water. This scene, which for most people contains the hint of some kind of lyrical beauty, is seen by Seurat with an almost inhuman detachment. How natural it would seem to accentuate the beauty of the naked forms by choice of pose or of lighting! How easy to mitigate the banality of boots and trousers! But here everything is given with the same even, unrelenting unemphatic precision of statement. There is no bias whatsoever. The hot haze of the summer afternoon whitens the luminous sky, half veils the distant factories and bridge, and plays over the luminous bodies in the foreground, and no one could render this enveloping with a more exquisitely tremulous sensibility, a more penetrating observation or more unfailing consistency, than Seurat; but, none the less, every contour of the ungainly shirt tucked into the half-drawn-up trousers, or of the boots and socks, is rendered with the same unchanging attention. Yet the effect is neither of lyric beauty, nor of banal or ironic realism. Seurat's aim lies behind and deeper than all such attitudes to the scene. It would be hard to find any word uncoloured enough to describe the mood this evokes. It is like that which comes to us from some of Piero della Francesca's monumental and motionless groups. It is a mood of utter withdrawal from all the ordinary as well as all the poetic implications of things into a region of pure and almost abstract harmony. For that, indeed, is the secret of this great composition, the compelling harmony of all these forms, the so evident inevitability of all its correspondences and correlations. Boots and trousers lose their everyday banality when they are implicated in so close-woven a texture of formal harmony, however relentlessly their shapes are defined. One is forced even to rejoice that boots have tabs, so evidently do they here become the key to a whole sequence of rhythmic phrasing. And no less does the beauty and charm of the summer sunshine sink into the background of consciousness and become only another part of the colour organization. But yet, in spite of the exactitude and rigour of its harmony, this picture retains also something of its quality of immediacy, of a thing that was actually seen and seized on by the imagination in a single ecstatic moment. It is just that quality that Seurat's passionate research for abstract principles and scientific method might, one guesses, endanger. With him the balance between sensibility and doctrine was a delicate one. If the doctrine were to cease to be amenable to constant correction by the sensibility it might become the predominant partner; demonstration would replace inspiration and theory passion. There was certainly a tendency for this to happen towards the end of Seurat's short life. That his sensibility would have regained the upper hand I do not doubt, but the balance sometimes inclines against it. The fact is that his method – he always called it '*ma méthode*', and any suggestion of infringement of his claim to have originated it moved him to something as near to self-assertiveness as his reserve and self-possession admitted – his method became increasingly his great passion, until he came to regard his pictures almost as demonstrations of its validity.

In the *Bathers* the method was not yet fully developed. The colour was put on in small dabs broken across by dabs of other colours, but those colours were always mixed on the palette to give the desired tint. He had not yet analysed the colours into more or less pure notes which should make up the required tint by means of optical mixture. Such a complete analysis implied, of course, much smaller units of colour, and this was finally attained by the juxtaposition of small round dots of the pure colours necessary to produce any required resultant.

The *Grande-Jatte* was the first application of the method in its amended and final form. It presents a world from which life and movement are banished, and all is fixed for ever in the rigid frame of its geometry. The *Poseuses* [now in the Barnes Collection, Merion, Pa., Fig. 6. The small version in the possession of Mr. Henry P. McIlhenny, is reproduced in colour, Plate 38], which was the most important work of the Lefèvre exhibition, follows closely on that. It is not so ambitious, but even more than with that, one feels that it has never quite been 'seen'. The *Grande-Jatte* was created by assembling innumerable separate studies, an assembly in which everything took its place according to the principles of harmony which Seurat had elaborated. In the *Poseuses* the same method is employed. Seurat has made the same model pose in back, side and front views in a corner of his room, one side of which is completely filled by his painting of the Grande-Jatte. One feels that the poses have been found in order to fit a preconceived geometric scheme. Certainly the position of every single object and every part of the contour of every object has been ascertained to an almost incredible nicety. One cannot move a button or a ribbon without disaster to this amazingly complete and closely knit system. Since Poussin surely no one has been able to design in such elaborate and perfect counterpoint. But I come back to my feeling that here the harmony has been arrived at almost by trial and error, by a perpetual adjustment and readjustment. I do not mean, of course, that such arrangement and adjustment of one thing to another was the result of any merely intellectual calculation. It needed in order to succeed nothing less than Seurat's impeccable sense of proportion, of quantities, of tone and colour values, and his marvellous sense of balance of direction. What I mean is that, none the less, one feels that at no moment did the rhythmic idea flash into the artist's consciousness as a melody suggests itself to a musician. Still there it is, a wonderfully strange and original composition almost disquieting in its fixity. It is a very epitome of its author's theories of analogy. The analogies run through it even to the minutest details, analogies of form and analogies of colour. In colour, for instance, the violets, greens and reds of the Grande-Jatte find their analogies in the wall, the mounted drawings and the green garment or bag so carefully hung upon it, and in the bright rust reds of the sofa and parasol.

The main idea of the composition is of two long uprights, one, the central nude, the other the seated nude prolonged into the two upright figures of the Grande-Jatte. The picture is thus divided exactly into two equal halves, a bold application of Poussin's favourite practice. One half is occupied by the Grande-Jatte, the other by the nearly blank wall at right angles to it. This right-hand half has, instead of a third upright, a pyramid into which the seated figure is almost forcibly fitted. The original idea of the central standing nude is to be seen in a very beautiful drawing published in M. Coquiot's book.* It was standing firm with both legs together. But Seurat felt the need of an analogy, in the left-hand half of the picture, to the pyramid in the right, and has made the model's right leg stick out so as to be almost exactly parallel with the left-hand side of his pyramid, in order to do so. There can be no doubt to my mind that this was right from the point of view of the perfection of the composition, but it has led to a certain meagreness in the drawing of this figure. The volumes here seem wanting in fullness, especially as compared with the surprising beauty and ease of the nude to the left. Just with regard to this central figure something too literal, something of the unassimilated fact, seems to have persisted. It lacks the great style of most of Seurat's drawing.

It is for such reasons that I cannot share the widely expressed opinion of my fellow critics that this is a greater masterpiece than the *Bathers*. It no doubt represents a further stage in the development of Seurat's method, but it is too much put together, it has lost something of the conviction and immediacy which had not yet been subordinated to his science when he did the *Bathers*, and which still persists in the landscapes of the last period. I cannot doubt that if he had lived Seurat would have found a way to put his completed method at the service of his sensibility. What revelations his early death deprived us of!

Certainly *Les Poseuses* shows once more that strange aloofness of Seurat's spirit which we noted in the *Bathers*; but it is less remarkable here where the

* *Seurat* by G. Coquiot, Paris 1924, plate opposite p. 160.

deliberate arrangement by the artist of the models in the studio gives already a certain air of unreality to the thing seen. But the same characteristic of Seurat's attitude awakens an almost disquieting feeling before the later *Jeune Femme se poudrant*, which was shown by Mr. Paul Rosenberg recently in London [Plate 42, now at the Courtauld Institute Galleries]. This is, indeed, one of the strangest pictures I know, so utterly remote is the point of departure from the place to which Seurat carries us. It is as though he had made a bet that he would take the most intractable material possible and yet mould it to his ends. This impossible woman, in the grotesque *déshabillé* of the 'eighties, surrounded by every horror of gimcrack finery of the period, might have inspired Daumier to a grim satire, or Guys to an almost lyrical delight in its exuberance, or Degas to a bitter and merciless epigrammatic exposure, or Lautrec to an indulgently ironical scherzo; but Seurat passes over all such implications with an Olympian indifference, he treats the subject with religious solemnity and carries it into a region of abstract beauty. No Byzantine mosaic, however solemnly hieratic, could be more remote than this from all suggestion of 'La vie Parisienne'. The design is affirmed with an almost oppressive decision. We are forbidden to imagine the slightest tremor of change in these impeccable contours. By incessant revision the position of everything has been ascertained down to the minutest fraction. At first it seems to be all surface – contours revealed by spots of pure but elusive colour – and then these almost imperceptible changes of colour build up for us solid volumes bathed in a faint glowing light. There is scarcely any tone contrast, no definite light and shade, and yet in the end these volumes assert themselves with overpowering completeness. For all its decorative flatness, for all its theoretical and abstract colouring, this is intensely real, but for all its reality nothing of the original theme, of the thing seen, remains untransformed, all has been assimilated and remade by the idea. And perhaps this complete transmutation of the theme by the idea is the test of great art. It means that in proportion as a picture attains to this independent reality and inherent significance the element of illustration drops out altogether and becomes irrelevant.

Near by, in the French Gallery, there hung a large composition of Picasso's, representing a 'Mother and Child', to which he had given colossal proportions and a preternatural massiveness of limb. To a prolonged gaze these seemed to become but airy trifles beside the immutable fixity of Seurat's woman.

The landscapes seen at the Lefèvre Gallery all belong more or less to the period of complete pointillism, though in some cases Seurat's earlier method of small swept brush strokes persists underneath the fine network of dots. Each in its entirely distinct way is, to my mind, a complete and irrefutable discovery. They are all

Fig. 2: WOMAN SEATED, HOLDING A PARASOL. Drawing, 1884–1885. New York, Museum of Modern Art

Fig. 3: PLOUGHING THE FIELDS. Drawing, about 1883. Paris, Louvre

Fig. 4: PORTRAIT OF AMAN-JEAN. Drawing, 1883. New York, Metropolitan Museum of Art

Fig. 5: A BATHER. Sketch for 'La Baignade', 1883–1884. Private Collection

Fig. 6: 'LES POSEUSES' Painting, 1886–1888. Merion, Pa., Barnes Foundation

primarily designs of specially conceived spaces filled by specially interpreted luminosities and colour vibrations. How perfect Seurat's insight was into such appearances and how nice his control of expression, can be realized when we compare the opalescent pearly greys of the *Courbevoie* [Plate 29, now in the Courtauld Institute Galleries] with the flaming whiteness of the *Gravelines* [now in the collection of Lord Butler] and the dither of sunlight in *Le Port* [Plate 44, now at the John Herron Art Institute, Indianapolis]. But as beautiful and surprising as any is the *Port-en-Bessin* [now in the Museum of Modern Art, New York], where the shadows of still clouds hanging over the sunlit sea make an exquisite arabesque, picked up again by the patterns of the turf on the weathered down in the foreground. When viewed at a short range this appears as an almost flat pattern design, but retire to the other end of the room and the planes stretch to infinite distances, with almost the effect of an illusion.

It is one of the peculiarities of the pointillist method that tones which are so near together as to be indistinguishable close at hand become strongly contrasted when viewed from farther off. It is this that enabled Seurat to keep the surface of his canvas so unaccented and yet to produce an almost exaggerated salience and depth of relief. Several of these landscapes have fortunately retained their original frames, flat pieces of wood covered by the artist with his interminable spots of colour. Again, we see his mastery of effects of contrast and his exacting logic. The argument, one sees, must have gone somewhat thus : the function of a frame is to cut off the imagined picture space from the actual space of the room. To do this there should be an equal contrast between frame and picture at every point. But with a gilt frame the contrast cannot be equal at every point. It is strong where the gilt comes against a dark mass in the picture, weaker where it opposes a light, not to mention the even greater differences of colour contrast which this uniform gold implies. Seurat, therefore, set to work so to paint the frame as that, at each point, both colour and tone contrasts should be equal, and one cannot deny that he has succeeded to perfection. Hardly less remarkable is the fact that a precisely similar technique in frame and picture produces in one case a solid flatness, in the other the illusion of recession and distance.

Seurat's artistic personality was compounded of qualities which are usually supposed to be opposed and incompatible. On the one hand, his extreme and delicate sensibility, on the other a passion for logical abstraction and an almost mathematical precision of mind. On the one hand he accepted the whole body of Impressionist discovery about appearance even to the point of stating those phenomena which, even while we observe them, we know to be illusory, on the other hand, the mere statement of appearance which so preoccupied the Impressionists has no importance whatever for him. Appearance as revealed by Impressionist researches is nothing to him but the raw material out of which he builds, and his building is so purely logical and architectural, so precisely balanced and so nicely proportioned that the final result is utterly remote from appearance. The question of verisimilitude hardly occurs to one, so little can we refer his pictures to anything outside themselves, so completely does the created reality hold us by the laws of its self-contained system.

No doubt, at all times in the history of art we find that newly discovered data of appearance become the basis for new ventures in design with a consequent modification and extension of the esthetic sensibility. What is rare and what makes Seurat's genius so surprising is that in the few years of his activity he was able, starting entirely *de novo* with the large body of new data which Impressionism supplied, together with his own additional observations on irradiation and the physiological effects of contrast, to create out of that, altogether afresh and without any guiding tradition so extraordinarily complete an esthetic system, together with a new technical method so perfectly adapted to its expression.

[This essay appeared in 'The Dial', Camden, N.J., in September 1926]

PLATES

1. MAN LEANING ON A PARAPET. Between 1881 and 1883. Ridgefield, Connecticut, Mr. Albert Roothbert

2. THE STONE-BREAKER. 1882. Washington, D.C., Phillips Collection

3. IN THE FOREST AT PONTAUBERT. 1881 (?), reworked later. Saltwood Castle, Sir Kenneth Clark

4. SUBURB. 1882. Troyes, M. Pierre Lévy

5. THE HORSE. About 1882. New York, Solomon R. Guggenheim Museum

6. HOUSES AT LE RAINCY. About 1882. Paris, Private Collection

7. THE WATERING-CAN. 1883. Upperville, Virginia, Mr. and Mrs. Paul Mellon

8. MAN PAINTING HIS BOAT. 1883. London, Lord Butler (Home House Trustees)

9. FIGURES IN A FIELD. About 1883. Private Collection

10. MAN FISHING FROM A MOORED BOAT. 1883. London, The Dowager Lady Aberconway

11. ANGLERS. 1883. Troyes, M. Pierre Lévy

12. HOUSE AMONG TREES. About 1883. Glasgow, City Art Gallery

13. HORSES IN THE RIVER. Study for 'Bathing at Asnières'. 1883–1884. London, The Dowager Lady Aberconway

14. BATHER SEATED. Study for 'Bathing at Asnières'. 1883–1884. Kansas City, The William Rockhill Nelson Gallery of Art

15. BATHING AT ASNIÈRES – 'UNE BAIGNADE'. 1883–1884, reworked about 1887. London, National Gallery

16. Detail of Plate 15

17. Detail of Plate 15

18. MAN FISHING. Study for 'Sunday afternoon on the Ile de La Grande-Jatte'. 1884–1885. London, The Dowager Lady Aberconway

19. COUPLE WALKING. Study for 'Sunday afternoon on the Ile de La Grande-Jatte'. 1884–1885. Tilton, Sussex, Lady Keynes

20. 'L'ILE DE LA GRANDE-JATTE'. 1884–1885. New York, Mr. John Hay Whitney

21. SUNDAY AFTERNOON ON THE ILE DE LA GRANDE-JATTE. 1883–1885, completed 1886. Chicago, Art Institute

22. Detail of Plate 21

23. THE RIVER SEINE AT COURBEVOIE. About 1885–1886. Paris, Private Collection

24. FIELD OF POPPIES. About 1884–1885. Maldon, Essex, Mrs. Pamela Diamand

25. 'LE BEC DU HOC, GRANDCAMP'. 1885. London, Tate Gallery

26. THE LIGHTHOUSE AT HONFLEUR. 1886. London, Mr. A. Chester Beatty

27. THE BEACH AT BAS-BUTIN, HONFLEUR. 1886. Tournai, Musée des Beaux-Arts

28. EVENING AT HONFLEUR. 1886. New York, Museum of Modern Art

29. THE BRIDGE AT COURBEVOIE. 1886–1887. London, Courtauld Institute Galleries (Home House Trustees)

30. 'LA MARIA', HONFLEUR. 1886. Prague, National Gallery

31. IN HONFLEUR HARBOUR. 1886. Otterlo, Kröller-Müller Museum

32. THE QUAY AT PORT-EN-BESSIN. 1888. Minneapolis, Institute of Arts

33. SUNDAY AT PORT-EN-BESSIN. 1888. Otterlo, Kröller-Müller Museum

34. THE EIFFEL TOWER. 1889. New York, Mr. and Mrs. Germain Seligman

35. MODEL STANDING. Study for 'Les Poseuses'. 1886–1887. Paris, M. Georges Renand

36. MODEL SEATED, PROFILE. Study for 'Les Poseuses'. 1886–1887. Paris, Louvre

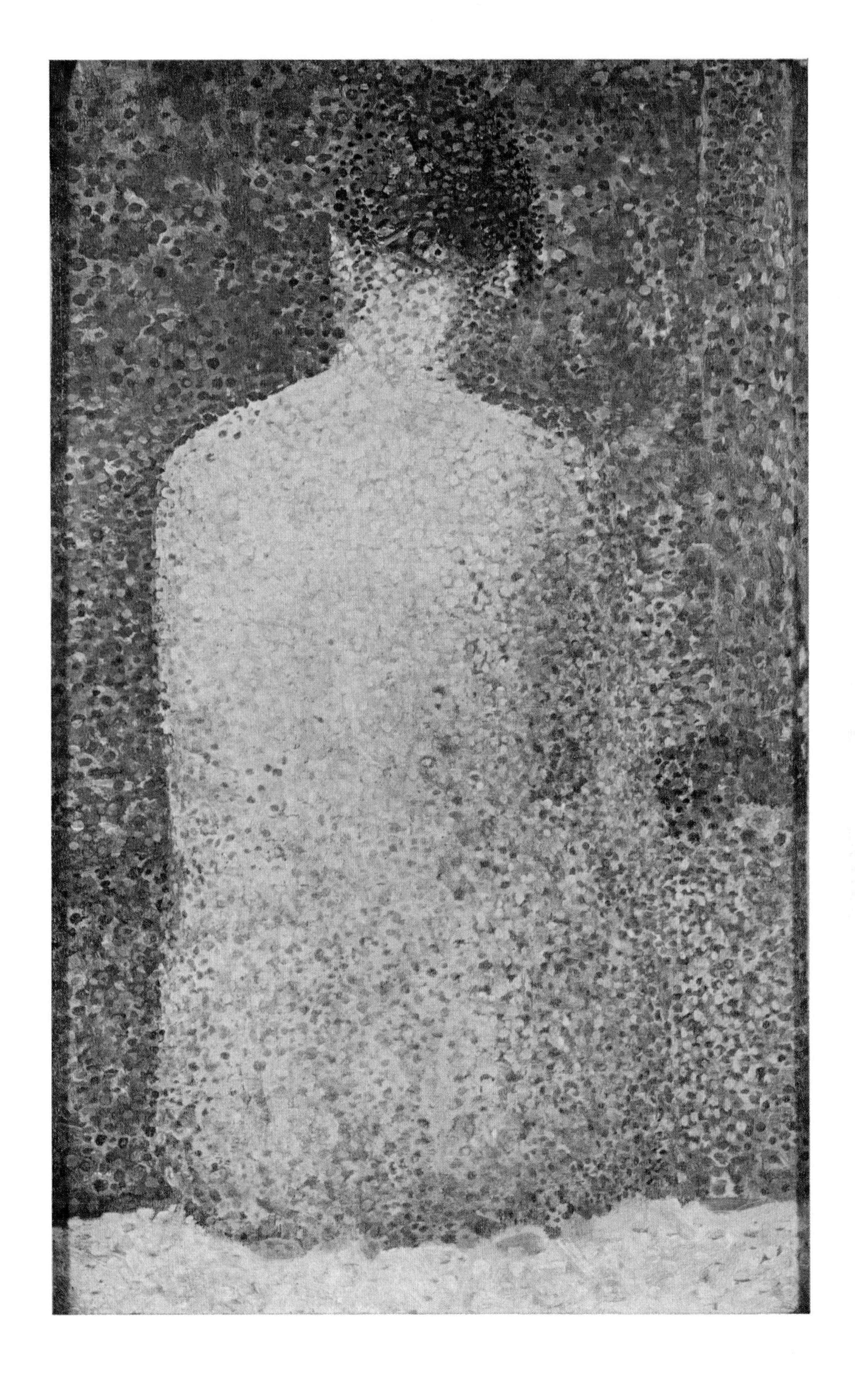

37. MODEL SEATED, BACK VIEW. Study for 'Les Poseuses'. 1886–1887. Paris, Louvre

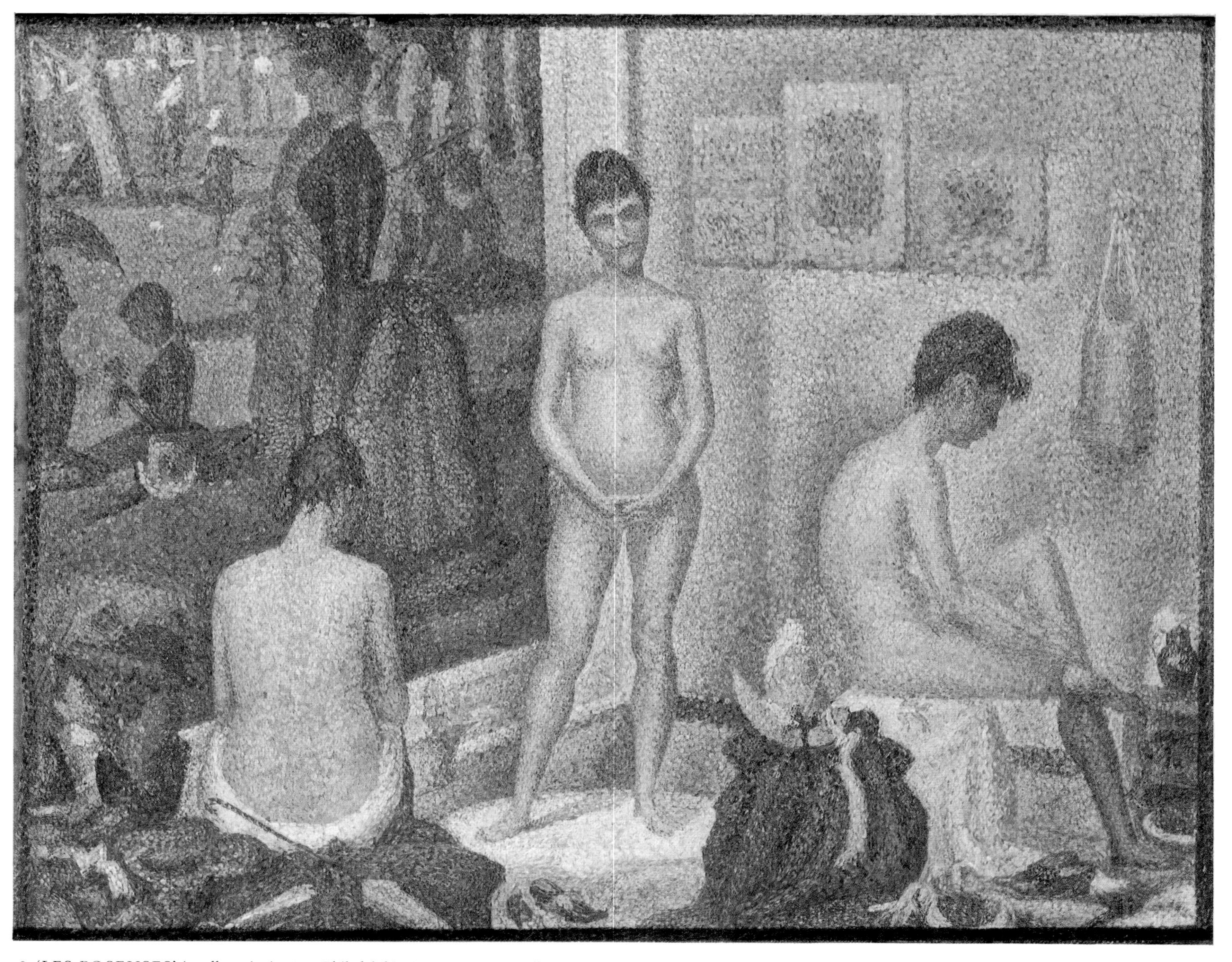

38. 'LES POSEUSES' (small version). 1888. Philadelphia, Mr. Henry P. McIlhenny

39. 'LA PARADE'. 1887–1888. New York, Metropolitan Museum of Art

40. Detail of Plate 39

41. STUDY FOR 'LE CHAHUT'. 1889–1890. London, Courtauld Institute Galleries (Home House Trustees)

42. WOMAN POWDERING HERSELF. Probably 1889–1890. London, Courtauld Institute Galleries (Home House Trustees)

43. 'LE CHAHUT'. 1889–1890. Otterlo, Kröller-Müller Museum

44. THE HARBOUR AT GRAVELINES. 1890. Indianapolis, The John Herron Art Institute

45. THE HARBOUR AT GRAVELINES, EVENING. 1890. New York, Mr. and Mrs. A. M. Burden

46. GRAVELINES. 1890. London, Courtauld Institute Galleries (Home House Trustees)

47. TREES AND BOATS. 1890. New York, Miss Alice Tully

48. THE CIRCUS. 1890–1891. Paris, Louvre

CHRONOLOGY
LETTER TO MAURICE BEAUBOURG
NOTES ON THE PLATES

CHRONOLOGY

Born 1859.

1878–79 Trained at the Beaux-Arts under Henri Lehmann, a pupil of Ingres.

1879 Military service at Brest.

1880 Working mainly in Paris and its suburbs.

1883 His drawing of his friend Aman-Jean (Fig. 4) is accepted for exhibition at the Salon.

1884 *Une Baignade à Asnières* refused by the Salon but exhibited at the Salon des Indépendants. Meets Signac.

May 1884 – March 1885 Paints *Un Dimanche à la Grande-Jatte.*

Summer 1885 Visits Grandcamp in Normandy and paints first seascapes.

October 1885 – Spring 1886 Reworks *La Grande-Jatte*, which is shown at the eighth Impressionist exhibition.

Summer 1886 Visits Honfleur at the mouth of the Seine.

Autumn 1886 – Spring 1887 Paints *Les Poseuses.*

Winter 1887 – 88 Paints *La Parade de Cirque*, which is shown with *Les Poseuses* at the Indépendants.

Summer 1888 Visits Port-en-Bessin on the Normandy coast.

Summer 1889 Visits Le Crotoy, near Abbeville.

Winter 1889 – 90 Paints *Jeune femme se poudrant* and *Le Chahut*, which are both shown at the Indépendants.

Summer 1890 Visits Gravelines, between Calais and Dunkerque.

Winter 1890 – 91 Works on *Le Cirque*, which is left unfinished, but shown at the Indépendants.

March 1891 Falls ill and dies within a few days (March 29th).

SEURAT'S LETTER TO THE WRITER BEAUBOURG

AUGUST 28, 1890

AESTHETIC

Art is Harmony. Harmony is the analogy of contrary and similar qualities in *tone*, *colour*, and *line*, considered with reference to a dominant and under the influence of a scheme of lighting in cheerful, calm or sad combinations.

The contraries are:

In *tone*, a { more luminous / lighter } against a darker.

In *colour*, the complementaries; that is, a particular red set against its complementary, etc. (red-green; orange-blue; yellow-violet).

In *line*, those that form a right-angle.

Cheerfulness of *tone* results from a luminous dominant; of *colour*, from a warm dominant; of *line*, from angles above the horizontal.

Calmness of *tone* results from a balance of dark and light; of *colour*, from a balance of warm and cold; of *line*, from a horizontal.

Sadness of *tone* results from a dark dominant; of *colour*, from a cold dominant; of *line*, from angles below the horizontal.

TECHNICAL

Assuming the phenomena of the duration of a light-impression on the retina of the eye—A synthesis necessarily follows. The means of expression is the optical mixture of tones and colours (local colour and the colour of the source of illumination; sunlight, lamplight, gaslight, etc.), that is of lights and reactions against light (shadows), in accordance with the law of *contrast*, gradation and irradiation.

The frame is in a harmony that opposes those of the tones, colours and lines of the picture.

ESTHÉTIQUE

L'art c'est l'Harmonie. L'Harmonie c'est l'analogie des contraires, l'analogie des semblables, de *ton*, de *teinte*, de *ligne*, considérés par la dominante et sous l'influence d'un éclairage en combinaisons gaies, calmes ou tristes.

Les contraires ce sont:

Pour le *ton*, un plus { lumineux / clair } pour un plus sombre.

Pour la *teinte*, les complémentaires, c'est-à-dire un certain rouge opposé à sa complémentaire, etc. (rouge-vert; orange-bleu; jaune-violet).

Pour la *ligne*, celles faisant un angle droit.

La gaieté de *ton*, c'est la dominante lumineuse; de *teinte*, la dominante chaude; de *ligne*, les lignes au dessus de l'horizontale.

Le calme du *ton*, c'est l'égalité du sombre et du clair; de *teinte*, du chaud et du froid et l'horizontale pour la *ligne*.

Le triste du *ton*, c'est la dominante sombre; de *teinte*, la dominante froide et de *ligne*, les directions abaissées.

TECHNIQUE

Etant admis les phénomènes de la durée de l'impression lumineuse sur la rétine.

La synthèse s'impose comme résultante. Le moyen d'expression est le mélange optique des tons, des teintes (de localités et de la couleur éclairante: soleil, lampe à pétrole, gaz, etc.), c'est-à-dire des lumières et de leurs réactions (ombres) suivant les lois du *contraste* de la dégradation de l'irradiation.

Le cadre est dans l'harmonie opposée à celles des tons, des teintes et des lignes du tableau.

Fig. 7. 'AU CONCERT EUROPÉEN'. Drawing, 1887–1888. New York, Museum of Modern Art

NOTES ON THE PLATES

1. MAN LEANING ON A PARAPET.
25×16,2 cm. Between 1881 and 1883. Ridgefield, Connecticut, Mr. Albert Roothbert.

This work, which is usually dated to 1881, when Seurat was twenty-two but was perhaps painted a year or two later, combines in a curious way features of his early training and of his very late style. In its subtle balance of dark and light masses it reveals what he had learnt in the previous year or two through his *conté crayon* drawings conceived in terms of value as opposed to outline. In its strictly geometrical harmony it derives from his own master Lehmann and through him goes back to Ingres and even to Poussin. Yet in its strange feeling of isolation and mystery it looks forward to the remoteness of *Parade* (Pl. 39) or the very late landscapes. The debt to Impressionism is limited to the use of relatively pure colour; and the general character of the work is actually opposed to Impressionist principles: natural forms are reduced to their simplest terms; there is no sense of atmosphere or changing light, but rather that feeling of frozen, static illumination which was to be such a marked feature of the very late landscapes painted at Gravelines. Seurat had conceived the basic ideas of his revolution against Impressionism even at this early stage in his career.

2. THE STONEBREAKER.
16,2×25,4 cm. 1882. Washington, D.C., Phillips Collection.

This picture belongs to a series of small panels painted mainly in 1882 which reveal Seurat's interest in themes taken from the lives of peasants and workmen. [The date 1884 has also been suggested.]
A generation earlier Courbet in France and Brett in England had treated precisely the theme of the Stonebreaker, but they did so in order to convey a positive social message. Millet had treated similar subjects in a gentler manner, sometimes slipping over into sentimentality. Pissarro gave to his sympathy for the poor a noble and almost monumental form. Seurat has something of the sympathy of Pissarro, but with a greater aloofness.
Technically it is curious to notice that the artist who was in the *Baignade* to create one of the most monumental paintings of the century should here lag behind Pissarro in this quality. Whereas in the latter's work brush-strokes follow and model the solid form, Seurat's broader treatment allows the expression of more movement and less mass.

3. IN THE FOREST AT PONTAUBERT – 'SOUSBOIS À PONTAUBERT'.
76,4×61 cm. 1881 (?), reworked later. Saltwood Castle, Sir Kenneth Clark.

This picture presents peculiar problems from the point of view of dating. In some ways it looks back to the works of an earlier generation, even to Corot's soft paintings of the *Souvenir de Mortefontaine* type, but in other respects it foreshadows the geometrical planning and the systematic brushwork of the artist's mature works. Many artists of the late nineteenth century, being unable to sell their canvases, kept them in their studios and reworked them, but not always in the same spirit. Cézanne, for instance, feeling that he had not completely 'realized' his sensation in front of nature, never regarded a picture as completely finished, but simply put it aside with the deliberate intention of taking it up again when the mood came upon him. Seurat, on the other hand, as far as one can judge, painted a picture, found it in his studio some time later, was dissatisfied with it, and repainted it partly or wholly in the manner which he had evolved in the interval. The effect is that, whereas Cézanne's paintings are obviously the result of prolonged but continuous thought and concentration, in the case of certain Seurats – for instance the *Baignade* – it is easy to detect different treatments in different parts of the canvas. In *Sousbois* on the other hand the artist seems to have reworked the whole canvas, with the result that there is some feeling of conflict between the general conception of the painting and its actual execution.

4. SUBURB.
32,4×40,6 cm. 1882. Troyes, M. Pierre Lévy.

The suburbs of Paris provided an endless stimulus to Seurat and to other artists in the 1880's, either through their human themes, as in the *Baignade* or the *Grande-Jatte*, or through their visually evocative forms, as in this picture. The white-walled houses, each with a single sloping roof, and the elongated factory chimney, looking like a campanile in a view of Venice by Guardi, are transformed by Seurat into a landscape which in its formal purity reminds one of Corot's views of Rome, while at the same time it assumes and exploits – in a personal way – all the ocular discoveries of Impressionism.

5. THE HORSE.
32,4×41 cm. About 1882. New York, Solomon R. Guggenheim Museum.

This is one of the earliest paintings in which there is at any rate a suggestion of Seurat's interest in reducing living beings to completely static forms. The painting of the horse itself shows a rejection – almost certainly conscious – of the brilliant observation of equine movements which had characterized the early race paintings of Degas and a return to an archaic, strictly lateral view of the animal, which is framed in an arch composed not of stone but of trees to which a stone-like fixity has been given. Technically however the painting is still executed in the free criss-cross pattern of strongly coloured strokes which characterize the paintings so far discussed.

6. HOUSES AT LE RAINCY.
24×17 cm. About 1882. Paris, Private Collection.

This and the *Watering Can* (Pl. 7) must both have been painted when Seurat visited his father, who lived at Le Raincy, a small village just south of Paris. *Houses* was probably executed in 1882, and once again Seurat is shown at the cross-roads: it is still Impressionist in its use of colour, but the design is held together firmly by the straight lines – vertical, horizontal and diagonal – of the houses. In its repetition of similar roof-shapes the picture reminds one of Cézanne more than is usual with Seurat's early works.
It was at Le Raincy that Seurat's father had a garden and a little house away from his family, where he rigged up an altar and, with the help of an old gardener, used to conduct his own peculiar brand of Catholic observance.

7. THE WATERING CAN
24,4×15,5 cm. 1883. Upperville, Virginia, Mr and Mrs Paul Mellon.

In this painting, which almost certainly dates from 1883, Seurat has taken a further step towards his mature style. The geometry of the design is more emphatic than in any of the works so far discussed, except the *Man leaning on a Parapet* (Pl. 1), which may well date from the same year. Even a comparison of these two paintings, however, shows an interesting difference. The *Man leaning on a Parapet* is designed entirely in rectangles, whereas the lower half of the *Watering Can* is conceived in terms of curves. The stone edge to the flower-bed is bent round to form a curious distortion of the foreground space of a kind which the artist was to use in his very late landscapes (cf. Pl. 44), and the handle of the can adumbrates the curly surface patterns made by the whip in *Le Cirque* (Pl. 48) and the flags in the *Port-en-Bessin* (Pl. 33). At the same time the artist is beginning to use a smaller and more regular touch than previously, particularly in the painting of the trees.

8. MAN PAINTING HIS BOAT.
15,8×24,7 cm. 1883. London, Lord Butler (Home House Trustees).

This and the following works show that, while in some of the paintings executed in 1883, such as the *Watering Can*, Seurat was moving towards his later style, both in design and in handling, in others he used a much looser construction of the whole and broad, rapid brush-strokes. In subject this scene leads up to the *Baignade* (Pl. 15) and the *Grande-Jatte* (Pl. 21), in that all three paintings display the occupations not of peasants or workmen but those of the smaller bourgeois busy with their boats, fishing, bathing, or just walking along the banks of the river. In treatment the paintings of this group vary to a remarkable degree. Some, like the *Man painting his Boat*, are sunny in atmosphere, with light tone, dominated by yellow-greens and pale blues which, like the handling, recall the late Manet. Others, such as Pls. 10 and 11, are more carefully designed to form a linear pattern on the surface of the picture, and are dominated by sombre colours and unusual *contre-jour* effects.

9. FIGURES IN A FIELD.
15,2×24,8 cm. About 1883. Private Collection.

The title usually given to this picture, 'Figures in a Field', is misleading, since the real theme is of people walking along the river bank or resting beside it. In the background, across the river, there appear the little one-storey houses so frequent in the suburbs of Paris. The theme of women with parasols walking in a landscape had been frequent with Courbet and with the Impressionists, but Seurat's treatment of the figures is more remote and detached than is the case with the earlier artists.

10. MAN FISHING FROM A MOORED BOAT.
16,5×24,8 cm. 1883. London, The Dowager Lady Aberconway.

Although Seurat's famous letter about the effects of rising and falling lines (see p. 75) was written much later than 1883, when this picture was painted, its composition, with the vertical of the standing man, the horizontals of the boat and the further bank, and the sloping lines of the fishing rod and the beam, seems to foreshadow the main ideas of the letter and to demonstrate a pattern which combines a feeling of calm with one of soothing pleasure.

11. ANGLERS.
16,2×24,8 cm. 1883. Troyes, M. Pierre Lévy.

This masterly little picture was shown in 1886 at the eighth Impressionist Exhibition, and was described in an anonymous review in *La République Française* as 'le bijou de l'exposition', which may well not have pleased some of the Impressionists proper, such as Monet, Renoir and Sisley, who had abstained from exhibiting, probably because of the inclusion of works by Seurat and Signac. It was also praised, rather strangely, for having nothing 'thick and muddy' like Seurat's pictures of the sea or Pissarro's skies. Here Seurat has achieved something of the timeless static effect characteristic of the *Baignade*, though the figures are still flat and shadowy compared with the massiveness of those in the later picture. In this painting the effect of calm is obtained mainly by the repetition of near-horizontal lines, which make a pattern as subtle as that in the *Man fishing* but less rigid.

12. HOUSE AMONG TREES.
16,5×25,4 cm. About 1883. Glasgow, City Art Gallery.

This is yet another example of Seurat's small compositions based on views in the suburbs of Paris. In this case the exact site is not known, but it has the character of the village of Le Raincy (cf. Pls. 6 and 7). As in Pl. 10 the composition is given an almost geometrical skeleton by the horizontals of the wall and, curiously enough, the shadow of the tree on the right, which play against the diagonals of the roofs, but Seurat is here still using the free criss-cross handling of his early paintings.

13–17. Bathing at Asnières

13. HORSES IN THE RIVER.
15,2×24,8 cm. 1883–1884. London, The Dowager Lady Aberconway.

14. BATHER SEATED.
17,5×26,4 cm. 1883–1884. Kansas City, The William Rockhill Nelson Gallery of Art.

15. BATHING AT ASNIÈRES – 'UNE BAIGNADE'.
201×301,5 cm. 1883–1884, reworked about 1887. London, National Gallery.

16 and 17. Details of BATHING AT ASNIÈRES.

The big canvas, reproduced in Pl. 15, was Seurat's first work on a monumental scale. It was refused by the Salon of 1884 but shown in the same year at the first exhibition of the Artistes Indépendants, where it aroused ridicule in most visitors but created a profound impression on some artists, particularly on Paul Signac, who met Seurat for the first time on this occasion.
Seurat had been at work on this composition for more than a year, and the care with which he developed it is proved by the fact that thirteen preparatory sketches in oil and a number of drawings for it survive. Some of these sketches, like Pl. 13, are primarily landscape studies, others, like Pl. 14, are concerned above all with the figure group.
The painting has been compared with the frescoes of Piero della Francesca for its calm and monumental grandeur, and it is now known that Seurat could have seen copies of these frescoes at the Ecole des Beaux-Arts. Among more recent artists the main inspiration seems to have been Puvis de Chavannes, though Seurat is painting a world of reality as opposed to that of classical mythology in which the figures of Puvis move.
A study of the small sketches shows with what infinite care and sensibility Seurat worked out the main lines of his composition, moving and changing the outline of the river bank, raising or lowering the level of the horizon, and trying out various placings of the figures. Certain themes, such as the horse being scrubbed in Pl. 13, only appear at an early stage and then vanish altogether. The basic pattern is, however, clear from the beginning, however much it may be modified. The skeleton is formed by the diagonal of the river bank and the horizontal of the distant line of the bridges and buildings, but within this framework the figures are adjusted with extreme subtlety. Some, like the youth sitting with his legs dangling in the water or the boy immersed in the river up to his waist, form the main verticals of the design, whereas others, like the man lying in the left foreground, or the two immediately above him, develop with subtle variations the diagonal theme.
In the drawings Seurat almost, for the first time, uses his fully developed technique of *conté crayon* softened with a stump to produce the massive volumes of the individual figures.
The oil sketches are mainly in a technique reminiscent of the paintings of 1882 and 1883 but slightly more regular and controlled (cf. for instance Pl. 13). The painting itself, however, reveals novelties. Much of the foreground and many parts of the figures, for instance the clothes of the man seated shown in Pl. 16, are treated in the familiar loose criss-cross technique, but the flesh of all the figures has a thicker impasto and is painted with much smaller touches, a method which leads up to Seurat's later style.
In the *Baignade* we have another instance of Seurat taking up a completed picture and reworking it at a later date. The little touches round and on the orange hat of the boy on the extreme right are in the full *pointilliste* style of the artist's last years and form a complete contrast to the technique of the composition as a whole.
The picture, though one of the great masterpieces of European painting and probably the painting by Seurat most generally admired today, is in a sense a transitional work. In its monumentality, its stillness and its feeling of silence it foreshadows features which were to be intensified in the later works, possibly to a too great extent, but in the *Baignade* Seurat's humanity is still evident and indeed fundamental to the whole conception of the picture, and there is no trace of that extreme intellectualism which, some may feel, gives a chill to his very last figure paintings.

18–22. Sunday Afternoon on the 'Ile de la Grande-Jatte'

18. MAN FISHING.
24,1×15,2 cm. 1884–1885. London, The Dowager Lady Aberconway.

19. COUPLE WALKING.
81,5×65,2 cm. 1884–1885. Tilton, Sussex, Lady Keynes.

20. 'L'ILE DE LA GRANDE-JATTE'.
65×81,5 cm. 1884–1885. New York, Mr John Hay Whitney.

21. SUNDAY AFTERNOON ON THE ILE DE LA GRANDE-JATTE.
207×308 cm. 1883–1885, completed 1886. Chicago, Art Institute.

22. Detail of Plate 21.

This, Seurat's second painting on a large scale, was mainly planned and executed between May 1884 and March 1885, but Seurat took it up again and reworked it during the winter and spring of 1885–86 after his visit to Grandcamp, where he painted the seascapes (cf. Pl. 25) in which he fully developed his new technique. It cost the artist even more time and pains than the *Baignade*, as can be judged by the surviving oil sketches, more than thirty in number, quite apart from a large series of drawings.

As with the *Baignade*, the studies are concerned with different aspects of the painting, principally the setting and the figure groups, but they show an even greater variety than those for the earlier painting. Seurat began by making a series of small studies of views on the river bank, all representing more or less the same site, but seen from different points and with different light effects, but, whereas with the *Baignade* the main outlines of the composition were fixed at a relatively early stage, with the *Grande-Jatte* the artist seems to have gone on experimenting with different arrangements for a much longer time. From the beginning he was evidently fascinated by the pattern made by the slender tree trunks cutting across the line of the river bank, and he tried out many variations with the trees differently spaced. Then the strong line of the shadow across the foreground becomes a settled feature of all the variations and the general pattern of the design is fixed. At this point Seurat records his ideas in a very unusual painting (Pl. 20), which shows the stage exactly as he was to use it in the finished picture, but devoid of figures. Meanwhile he had been studying the figures which were ultimately to people the scene. His preparations took the form of a number of small but rapid oil sketches of individual figures (Pl. 18) or groups of figures (Pl. 19), and of very careful drawings not only of the people but of details such as the monkey that accompanies the couple on the right.

The final painting is even more accomplished than the *Baignade*. The massive simplicity of the latter has given place to a refinement of linear balance which is incidentally appropriate to the greater elegance of the subject. Here we see for the first time that finality which has always been singled out as a feature of Seurat's art, the impression that it would be impossible to move any line or mass without throwing out the harmony of the whole. In this context it is significant that Seurat should have marked a passage in a volume by the aesthetician David Sutter which read: 'In Greek art everything is foreseen with taste, feeling and complete science. No detail is left to chance; everything is related to the mass by the play of aesthetic lines.'

In the *Grande-Jatte* the geometry is more austere than in the *Baignade* and, apart from the river bank, there is hardly a diagonal in the whole picture; instead the design is made up of verticals in trees and figures or little curves in parasols and in the tails of the dogs and the monkey which are almost *art nouveau* in their forms.

Seurat has made as great advances in technique as in compositional method. Whereas in the *Baignade* he was still using a technique which was basically a variation of Impressionism – however different the purpose for which it was used – in the *Grande-Jatte* he applied the full method of what he called colour-luminism but has come to be generally known as Divisionism or Pointillism, based on a study of colour far more self-conscious and more scientific than had ever been attempted by the Impressionists. Basing himself largely on the optical discoveries of Chevreul, Seurat aimed at analysing the colour of an object into the following elements:

1. The colour that the object would have in white light, i.e. its local colour.
2. The colour of the light falling on it, e.g. a warm yellow if the object is in sun-light.
3. The colour created by that part of the light falling on the object which is modified by the colour of the latter before being reflected from it.
4. Light reflected on the object from other coloured objects near it.
5. Colour induced by the contrast with neighbouring objects, e.g. an object seen against the sky will take on something of the colour complementary to blue, namely orange.

In a sense these principles were only a scientific formulation of ideas which had been perceived by earlier painters such as Delacroix, Manet and the Impressionists, but it is in accordance with Seurat's essentially intellectual approach that he should have wished to give them a form derived from recent scientific discoveries in the field of optics.

In putting these theories into practice Seurat applied – but more rigidly – the Impressionist principle of using pure colours and allowing the mixture to be made in the spectator's eye, and his 'system' involved abandoning the broad and free brush-stroke of the early works and replacing it by a series of minute dots of colour, a technique which sacrifices any expressive use of handling which the Impressionists still acknowledged.

This method is not applied to the whole area of the *Grande-Jatte*; plate 21 shows that in many parts of the middle distance and background, particularly in the water – no doubt the areas left unaltered when Seurat reworked the painting in 1885–86 – he still uses a soft, delicate touch which owes much to Renoir; but in the figures seated in the foreground there is no concession: they are rigidly drawn and painted according to the new system. In the couple on the right, however, the appeals to the intellect and the eye are reconciled in an almost miraculous manner; the purples and the blacks of the woman's dress are painted according to Seurat's scientific procedure, but they have a velvety richness which proves that Seurat could, if he had wished, have given his paintings a sensuous beauty worthy of a Venetian. Unhappily this texture is something which cannot be conveyed in a small reproduction, in which a painting

more than six feet high has inevitably to be reduced to as many inches.
The finished study for the landscape setting, reproduced on Pl. 20, shows a good example of the painted frames which Seurat made for his pictures (cf. above, p. 21). An even more elaborate example is to be seen on Pl. 28.

23. THE SEINE AT COURBEVOIE.
81,5×65 cm. About 1885–1886. Paris, Private Collection.

This small composition is close in spirit and technique to the first stage of the *Grande-Jatte* and was no doubt painted at the same period; but in design it has something of the strict vertical and horizontal geometry of the big picture in its finished state.
Seurat here employs a method of composition which he was to use with great effect later, the balancing of heavy masses against empty space, in this case the trees on the right against the sheet of water and the shaded foreground on the left, a plane surface broken only by the slender, elongated figure of the woman, a tiny paper silhouette without weight or bulk, and her even tinier dog, which darts forward and provides the only movement in an otherwise entirely still design.

24. THE FIELD OF POPPIES.
64×81 cm. About 1884–1885. Maldon, Essex, Mrs Pamela Diamand.

The dating of this picture has given rise to much discussion, but it was probably painted about 1884–85. The criss-cross handling is still in the manner of the paintings executed in 1883 and the high horizon, an unusual feature in Seurat's paintings, is to be found in the study for the landscape setting of the *Grande-Jatte* (Pl. 20). The painting is probably one of the works by Seurat which influenced Van Gogh, who wrote about the artist with enthusiasm to his brother Theo during his time in Paris in 1886–1888.
The *Poppies* belonged to Roger Fry, who bought it in Paris between 1920 and 1922. It would have appealed to him as an example of the artist's style before it had reached its most doctrinaire stage.

25. 'LE BEC DU HOC, GRANDCAMP'.
64,5×81,5 cm. 1885. London, Tate Gallery.

In the summer of 1885 Seurat went to spend some weeks at Grandcamp in Normandy, near the Cherbourg peninsula, where he painted his earliest seascapes. These include many slight sketches like the *croquetons* painted in 1882–84, but one of the few larger canvases executed at this time, the *Bec du Hoc*, shows a new approach towards landscape. Seurat has evidently been fascinated by the strange shape of the rock jutting out into the sea, and in order to render its character he breaks abruptly with his previous method of design. He throws aside the geometrical grid of horizontals and verticals which had dominated not only the *Grande-Jatte* but also the *Seine at Courbevoie*, and works instead in terms of masses and lines curving into space, both lines and masses being provocatively broken at their extreme point by the sharp line of the horizon, over which hover – for one cannot really believe that they are flying – five sea-birds.
It may be felt that this painting is a bold experiment rather than a perfectly satisfactory work of art, but it undoubtedly marks a turning point in Seurat's development. His rejection of his previous methods of design in landscape opened up the way to the great works of his very last years. This painting is also important as one of the first examples of his use of the full Divisionist technique, since it was painted before he reworked the *Grande-Jatte* in the winter of 1885–86.
The landscapes painted at Grandcamp are also important from another point of view. Hitherto in Seurat's painting nature had been treated as a setting for man, and the artist's compositions had shown either man pursuing his normal occupations in the countryside or by the river, or nature as organized by man into gardens or fields. In some of the Grandcamp landscapes, such as the *Bec du Hoc*, man disappears altogether, and Seurat seems actually to take pleasure in representing an aspect of nature untamed by man.

26–28, 30, 31. Landscapes of Honfleur

26. THE LIGHTHOUSE AT HONFLEUR.
65×81,5 cm. 1886. London, Mr A. Chester Beatty.

27. THE BEACH AT BAS-BUTIN, HONFLEUR.
66×82 cm. 1886. Tournai, Musée des Beaux-Arts.

28. EVENING AT HONFLEUR.
78,8×94,2 cm. 1886. New York, Museum of Modern Art.

30. 'LA MARIA', HONFLEUR.
52,6×63,5 cm. 1886. Prague, National Gallery.

31. IN HONFLEUR HARBOUR.
79,5×63 cm. 1886. Otterlo, Kröller-Müller Museum.

In the summer of 1886, after completing the *Grande-Jatte* and seeing it shown at the eighth Impressionist exhibition, Seurat spent some time at Honfleur, a port at the mouth of the Seine. Here he painted a few pictures of sea and coast in a style based on his experiments of the previous year. In the *Beach at Bas-Butin* (Pl. 27), for instance, the cliffs on the right form strange shapes, like the *Bec du Hoc*, and the whole design is based on the balance of the solid rocks against the empty space of the sea, across which the trawler and the sailing boats move like the woman with her dog in the *Seine at Courbevoie*. But Seurat was as much fascinated by the port as by the rocky coast. In *Evening at Honfleur* (Pl. 28) he uses the breakwaters to form a pattern of repeated diagonals, steadied by the quite arbitrarily simplified horizontal forms of the clouds. The strongly vertical lines of the lighthouse, cutting orthogonally across the horizontals of the pier and the jetty, provided a stimulating theme for the type of planned landscape at which Seurat was already proficient (Pl. 26), but in the harbour itself he found themes of a new kind in the subtly curving lines of rigging playing against the straight lines of masts and quays. In *Honfleur Harbour* (Pl. 31) he has evolved from the repetitions of these forms a surface pattern which already evokes the complexity of *Le Chahut* (Pl. 43), though based on totally different subject matter.

29. THE BRIDGE AT COURBEVOIE.
45,8×54,6 cm. 1886–1887. London, Courtauld Institute Galleries (Home House Trustees).

During the winter of 1886–87 Seurat's main preoccupation was with the *Poseuses* (Pls. 35–38), but it was probably at this time that he painted the *Pont de Courbevoie*, one of his most harmonious and easy landscapes.
The lay-out of the picture is given by the landscape setting, which follows the *Baignade* in its general scheme – the diagonal of the river bank crossed by the horizontal of the bridge and buildings in the distance – and the careful spacing of the masts is a sort of scientific variation on the pattern of tree-trunks in the *Grande-Jatte*; but the artist has combined these elements of his earlier manner with a use of the Divisionist technique even more systematic than in the *Grande-Jatte*, and with a detachment in regard to the human elements which verges on contempt. The figures are smaller in relation to the landscape than in most of the earlier works, but this is not the essential difference. In the *Seine at Courbevoie* the only human figure was minute but had a certain character, even a certain dignity, as a human being. Here the figures are mere puppets, without life or reality, whose only function is to form parallels with the lines of the poles or contrasts to them by their differing angle or their greater width in silhouette.

32–33. Landscapes at Port-en-Bessin

32. THE QUAY AT PORT-EN-BESSIN.
64,9×82,4 cm. 1888. Minneapolis, Institute of Arts.

33. SUNDAY AT PORT-EN-BESSIN.
66×82 cm. 1888. Otterlo, Kröller-Müller Museum.

In the summer of 1888, after completing *Les Poseuses* and *La Parade*, Seurat made yet another excursion to the sea, this time to Port-en-Bessin, a little to the east of Grandcamp. One of the views painted there (Pl. 32) may be considered as a direct continuation of the style employed by the artist in the *Bridge at Courbevoie:* strict geometrical balance, careful planning of verticals – notice the curious placing of the bollards in the middle of the composition – strict application of the Divisionist technique, and the reduction of the human beings to puppets; but there is a brightness in the colour, particularly in the strong yellows, not to be found in the paintings of the previous years. This gaiety – very unusual with Seurat – is repeated in the *Sunday at Port-en-Bessin* (Pl. 33), not only in the colour but in the gay curves of the flags which flutter across the top left-hand corner of the painting. In the *Quay at Port-en-Bessin* Seurat begins to use the kind of blank, open foreground which was to be so effective in the landscapes painted at Gravelines in the last summer of his life.

34. THE EIFFEL TOWER.
24,1×15,2 cm. 1889. New York, Mr and Mrs Germain Seligman.

The Eiffel Tower, which was completed by the summer of 1889 for the International Exhibition held in Paris that year, was the subject of great disagreement between the different factions in the art world. To the Beaux-Arts it was a symbol of all that was vulgar in the industrialized life of modern times; to their opponents it represented a triumph of science and a resolution of the conflict between architecture and engineering. The fact that Seurat painted it before it was even finished – the top storey is incomplete – proves that in this, as in so many cases, he was on the side of progress and against the reactionary views of the Beaux-Arts. In its bright colours and its curves the picture carries on the gaiety of the Port-en-Bessin landscape paintings.

35–38. 'Les Poseuses'

35. MODEL STANDING.
25,4×16,2 cm. 1886–1887. Paris, M. Georges Renand.

36. MODEL SEATED, PROFILE.
25×15,9 cm. 1886–1887. Paris, Louvre.

37. MODEL SEATED, BACK VIEW.
24,5×15,5 cm. 1886–1887. Paris, Louvre.

38. 'LES POSEUSES' (small version).
39,4×48,9 cm. 1888. Philadelphia, Mr Henry P. McIlhenny.

The lightness and gaiety of the landscapes just discussed is also to be felt in Seurat's next large-scale figure composition, *Les Poseuses*, planned and executed between the autunm of 1886 and the spring of 1888. The final painting in the Barnes Collection, Merion, Pa., is unfortunately not available for reproduction in colour but is reproduced in black and white (fig. 6) and Pl. 38 shows the exquisite small version belonging to Mr McIlhenny, which has all the qualities of the full-size canvas. Plates 36 and 37 give the small studies for two of the figures, and Pl. 35 shows the surprisingly free first sketch for the central nude.
Roger Fry writes at some length of the *Poseuses* in his essay on Seurat, printed as an introduction to this book (see above, pp. 14–15), and there is little to add to his admirable analysis.

39–40. 'LA PARADE'.
99,7×150 cm. 1887–1888. New York, Metropolitan Museum of Art.

This picture, painted in the winter of 1887–88, was the subject of a brilliant essay by Roger Fry, of which the following paragraphs are the essential parts:

In a hundred different ways critics have tried to express a peculiar feeling which great works of art arouse – the feeling, I mean, of their isolation from all else, the feeling that the great work of art exists and persists by its own internal coherence rather than by its references to what lies outside of it – that it is, as it were, a self-conditioned, self-subsistent organism, containing within itself, if anywhere, the justification for each part of it being what it is. But even the purest and most abstract work of art has some references to the surrounding world of actual life. At the very least it derives somewhere from an experience which occurred to the artist in that world. This would be true, for instance, of the purest music ever invented, but for the painter it is almost certain that not only did the artist's original experience occur in the actual world but that a great number of visual data will have entered into that experience, and being an essential part thereof will have passed over into the work of art. These visible data, these facts of appearance, will, indeed, probably tell us what the picture is *about*, in the crude, external sense; tell us what kind of a scene is represented, what, in short, the title of the picture is likely to be. But the relation of these visible facts to the final result, to the essential meaning of the picture, is by no means a fixed one. It requires, sometimes, a great deal of tact to find the way from one to the other. Indeed, I suspect that it is somewhere in this passage that the majority of gross mistakes in appreciation are made. It is somewhere on the way between the ostensible external appearance and the innermost significance of the forms that so many people, including critics, occasionally trip up. It is probably some difficulty in the relation between these two terms that causes those long delays in the recognition of certain artists and that, even when they have once been recognized, may at any time deprive them of critical or popular esteem.

Seurat's picture of *La Parade* is an instance of how complicated and unexpected this relation of external facts and ultimate meaning may be. For it would be hard to find another instance of a greater stretch between the two terms involved. On the one hand, at the terminus *a quo* we have facts, the most minutely – one might say trivially – particular, facts of a photographic literalness, and at the other – at the terminus *ad quem* – something as abstract, as universal and as unconditioned as pictorial art ever attained to, at least, before the days of cubism. Almost all other works of art find both point of departure and point of arrival in some intervening region between the two that Seurat has chosen. Thus one can scarcely think of any other artist since primitive times who would accept such minute visual data as Seurat does in the dressed-up page-boy or in the profiles and hats of the crowd. It is this precision in what is most unessential and momentary that is so surprising. And this is so marked that I suppose anyone familiar with the details of late nineteenth century costume would be able to date this picture to within a year or so by the evidence of these profiles.

From this point of view it is interesting to put side by side Seurat and his contemporary, Toulouse-Lautrec. Both frequented Montmartre and saw similar sights, both might have stopped outside the same circus somewhere in the Boulevard Clichy. Toulouse-Lautrec would have seized at once on all that was significant of the moral atmosphere, would have seized most of all on what satisfied his slightly morbid relish of depravity, with just too little of detachment for irony but not for an amused and half-disdainful complicity. No shade of all that such indications would have meant to an alert and initiated Parisian would have escaped him and he would have woven therefrom something that had, after all, a kind of lyrical glamour. But Seurat, one feels, saw it almost as one might suppose some visitant from another planet would have done. He saw it with this penetrating exactness of a gaze vacant of all direct understanding. Form after form he notes down with a more rigid precision than his contemporary's brilliant impressionist shorthand could ever attain to. The turn of a feather in a hat went exactly so, a nose stuck out under the hat brim at just that angle, a bowler hat fitted on to a head in just that improbable way; but he noted all with this gaze that refused to see any implications other than visual elements in a scheme of fixed and abstract perfection. Each figure seems to be so perfectly enclosed within its simplified contour, for, however precise and detailed Seurat is, his passion for geometricizing never deserts him – enclosed so completely, so shut off in its partition, that no other relation than a spatial and geometrical one is any longer possible. The syntax of actual life has been broken up and replaced by Seurat's own peculiar syntax with all its strange, remote and unforeseen implications. For these figures have nothing left of the life of the Boulevard Clichy. A magician's wand has made out of momentary poses an eternal monument. That moment of hurried life, of bustle and eagerness, of excitement, anticipation and noise has become transfigured into something of more than Egyptian, more than hieratic, solemnity and stillness. It would give a wrong impression to say that the life of the instant had been arrested, or frozen, for there is nothing momentary in any of the forms however momentary the pose from which they are taken.

It is as though Seurat had not only painted the 'Grecian urn' but had written Keats's poem on it all in a single action for, certainly, here far more than in any Grecian urn and without external aid, we feel that 'this silent form doth tease us out of thought as doth eternity'. Even among Seurat's works this picture seems to me to be unique in the completeness with which the most literal facts of everyday life have been transmuted into the purest, most abstract of spiritual values.

This transmutation results from the extreme simplification of all the forms according to certain conscious and deliberate principles. Thus we note that across the elaborate rectilinear framework of the design are played two main formal elements, an ovoid exemplified in the two blue patches on the *affiche* repeated in the numbers behind the central figure and again and again in the bowler hats and shoulders of the men and, in contradiction to this, the conical shapes of the trombone-player's head and hat, inverted in his legs and again in several of the women's hats. It is perhaps this continuous repetition of a few simple forms that gives to the picture its strange fixity and stillness.
No less important, however, in bringing about that transmutation of the actual scene is the rigorous counterpoint which controls their relations in the picture space. In this, indeed, one seems to see something almost like a direct influence of Poussin. Here, as before a Poussin, we recognize a perfect harmonic treatment of intervals – an impeccable sense for the relative proportions of parts. As in Poussin, the centre line is deliberately accented by the central figure and by the rigid vertical made by his trombone carried so wilfully down one side of his leg; and as in some of his works there is a sharply marked difference in the building up of the two counterpoised halves. But it would be foolish to press this comparison far, for however similar the underlying methods of composition may be, the temperament of these two are very distinct and the moods each expressed are utterly diverse. For Poussin had nothing of the peculiar tenderness of Seurat, nothing of his tremulous anxiety about the quality of his forms nor his almost religious respect and delicacy of feeling. But they share alike a rare passion for the significance of abstract and architectural formal harmonies.
[*Burlington Magazine*, LV, 1929, July–December, pp. 289 ff.]

41, 43. 'Le Chahut'

41. STUDY FOR 'LE CHAHUT'.
21,5×16,5 cm. 1889–1890. London, Courtauld Institute Galleries (Home House Trustees).

43. 'LE CHAHUT'.
169,1×139 cm. 1889–1890. Otterlo, Kröller-Müller Museum.

This painting, one of Seurat's strangest works, was planned and carried out in the winter of 1889–90. It is the antithesis of the early pictures like the *Baignade* and *La Grande-Jatte*, in which man is seen as living in a sort of harmony with nature, even if it was only the nature of the Paris suburbs. In the later landscapes nature dominates and man is reduced to a subordinate role. In *Le Chahut* as in *La Parade* the artist deals with human activities, but of the most sophisticated kinds, far removed from the almost naïve atmosphere of the two early masterpieces. The remote dream-like stillness of *La Parade* is replaced by a riot of noise and movement, and the scene takes place in a stifling room lit by gas lamps which make *art-nouveau* patterns on the wall in the background. True, the movement is frozen and the sound can only be deduced, but the violence of both is none the less evident for that.
Plate 43 reproduces the large painting in the Kröller-Müller collection, whereas Pl. 41 shows the small sketch in the Courtauld Institute Galleries, which has unfortunately lost the painted surround on the right-hand side, together with a small part of the painting itself. Originally, no doubt, the figures on this side were complete as they are in the big picture.

42. WOMAN POWDERING HERSELF.
94,5×79,2 cm. Probably 1889–1890. London, Courtauld Institute Galleries (Home House Trustees).

This picture was probably painted in 1889–90, though Signac, who knew the artist intimately, stated that it was executed earlier, in 1888–89. It represents Madeleine Knobloch, with whom Seurat had been living for some time and by whom he had had a son. A tradition, apparently going back to the artist's life-time, had it that the artist originally painted his own portrait in the frame on the wall which now shows a pot of flowers on a table, but that a friend persuaded him that it would be indelicate for him to appear in such a manner. The truth of the legend was proved when, some years ago, the painting was X-rayed. There were clear traces of a different painting underneath the still-life, but unfortunately the artist had scraped out the original version so thoroughly that, though it was possible to say that it had probably represented a head, the remains were so vague as to be unintelligible in a photograph. When the picture was exhibited at Chicago in 1958, attempts were made to reconstruct the head, but they depended more on the ingenuity of the student who made the reconstruction than on the evidence revealed by the X-ray.
Once again we may refer to Fry's essay (see above, p. 16) for an analysis of this picture.

44–47. Landscapes at Gravelines

44. THE HARBOUR AT GRAVELINES.
73×92,7 cm. 1890. Indianapolis, The John Herron Art Institute.

45. THE HARBOUR AT GRAVELINES, EVENING.
65,3×82 cm. 1890. New York, Mr and Mrs W. A. M. Burden.

46. GRAVELINES.
15,9×24,8 cm. 1890. London, Courtauld Institute Galleries (Home House Trustees).

47. TREES AND BOATS.
15,9×25,4 cm. 1890. New York, Miss Alice Tully.

Roger Fry points out that in his last figure paintings Seurat seemed to be almost strangled by his own method. He adds that, if he had lived, he would no doubt have found a way out of this impasse.

It could be argued that he already found the solution to his problem in the last landscapes, painted at Gravelines, between Calais and Dunkirk, in the summer of 1890. These are among the strangest landscapes ever produced. They show scenes of human activity, but without a single man or woman being present; they depict air and sea and sailing ships, but without the slightest suggestion of movement; they are built up of large empty areas, but are filled with a sort of vibrant excitement. Strangest of all, however, is the treatment of light. The scene is usually shown in strong sunlight – Pl. 45 is an exception in depicting an evening scene – and, as Seurat chooses his point of view so that there shall be the minimum of shadow, the whole surface of the picture is in light; and yet, perhaps partly because of the absence of contrast with shaded parts, one does not have the feeling of a scene warmed by sun. The sandy foregrounds – in Pl. 44, for instance, and in the other paintings of the *Chenal* – seem almost to give off their own light; instead of being sun-drenched, they are glaring and almost incandescent. The stillness of the light is the counterpart of a stillness of scene and design more marked than ever before in Seurat's landscape painting. In Pl. 44 the eye is led into the picture by the disquietingly distorted foreground, but in most of the other finished paintings of this group there is hardly any break from the strict grid of horizontals and verticals. In the *croquetons* the method is the same, and Pl. 46 could be regarded as Seurat's most complete statement of his concept of the 'empty' landscape. (It should be thought of as slightly cooler in colour than it now appears, since it is now covered with a yellow varnish which unfortunately cannot be removed.)

48. The Circus

Frontispiece: STUDY FOR 'THE CIRCUS'.
55×46 cm. 1890. Paris, Musée d'Art Moderne.

48. THE CIRCUS.
186×151,1 cm. 1890–1891. Paris, Louvre.

This was the last of Seurat's large-scale compositions and was left unfinished at his death in the spring of 1891. In theme it continues *La Parade* and *Le Chahut*, but it is less like a pipe-dream than the former and less maenadic than the latter.
The foreground is laid out in a wide curve, like the edge of the quay in the *Harbour at Gravelines* (Pl. 44), and above it the lines of the benches form one of those networks of subtly varied curves with which Seurat had experimented in *Honfleur Harbour* (Pl. 31) and which he had perfected in *Le Chahut*. The element of *art nouveau* patterning which was first visible in the *Grande-Jatte* and gave such mystery to the gas-lamps in *La Parade* now jumps to the foreground and plays a much greater part in the fantastic silhouette of the clown, the curves of the whip, and the outlines of the two acrobats. *The Circus* is essentially a product of the 'nineties, but it could be used as text-book example to show the features that link the art of this period with certain aspects of sixteenth-century Mannerism. The distortions of space, the repetition of curves, the frozen movement, and the cut-off figures intruding into the foreground could all be paralleled in sixteenth-century painting; and the analogy is not limited to formal factors such as these: the atmosphere of sophistication and artificiality is so like certain works produced for the late Medici in Florence or their relatives in France that one is tempted to ask: Is this not the court-art of the late nineteenth-century bourgeoisie?
In connection with *The Circus*, and indeed with all Seurat's large-scale paintings from the *Grande-Jatte* onwards, attempts have been made to prove that his compositions were worked out on a system of intervals based on the Golden Section or some other simple relation. It is no doubt true that Seurat was interested in the speculation about these mathematical laws of beauty which were widespread in his time, but the attempts that have been made to analyse his paintings in these terms have always involved approximations so vague that they invalidate the demonstration. That Seurat was deeply concerned with precise harmony and balance is obvious; that he measured his designs out with ruler and compass is much less probable.

Fig. 8. THE ARTIST IN HIS STUDIO. Drawing, about 1884. Philadelphia, Museum of Art

LIST OF COLLECTIONS

ACKNOWLEDGEMENTS

The Publishers wish to thank private owners and public galleries for permission to reproduce the works in their collections. The publishers also wish to acknowledge with gratitude the permission given to them by Mrs Pamela Diamand and Messrs Chatto & Windus to reprint the essay on Seurat by Roger Fry.